THE ROMANIAN AMERICANS

THE ROMANIAN AMERICANS

Arthur Diamond

CHELSEA HOUSE PUBLISHERS

New York   New Haven   Philadelphia

Cover Photo: A Romanian-American family poses outside the Holy Trinity Romanian Orthodox Church in Youngstown, Ohio, on July 4, 1921.

Editor-in-Chief: Nancy Toff
Executive Editor: Remmel T. Nunn
Managing Editor: Karyn Gullen Browne
Copy Chief: Juliann Barbato
Picture Editor: Adrian G. Allen
Art Director: Giannella Garrett
Manufacturing Manager: Gerald Levine

Staff for THE ROMANIAN AMERICANS:
Senior Editor: Sam Tanenhaus
Assistant Editor: Abigail Meisel
Copyeditor: Karen Hammonds
Deputy Copy Chief: Ellen Scordato
Editorial Assistant: Theodore Keyes
Picture Researcher: PAR/NYC
Designer: Noreen M. Lamb
Layout: Louise Lippin
Production Coordinator: Joseph Romano
Cover Illustrator: Paul Biniasz
Banner Design: Hrana L. Janto

First Printing

1 3 5 7 9 8 6 4 2

Library of Congress Cataloging in Publication Data

Diamond, Arthur.
  Romanian Americans.

  (The Peoples of North America)
  Bibliography: p.
  Includes index.
  Summary: Discusses the history, culture, and religion of the Romanians, factors encouraging their emigration, and their acceptance as an ethnic group in North America.
  1. Romanian American—Juvenile literature.
[1. Romanian Americans] I. Title. II. Series.
E184.R8D5 1988   973'.0459   87-26822
ISBN 0-87754-898-6

CONTENTS

THE PEOPLES OF NORTH AMERICA

CHELSEA HOUSE PUBLISHERS

A
NATION
OF
NATIONS

Daniel Patrick Moynihan

The Constitution of the United States begins: "We the People of the United States . . ." Yet, as we know, the United States is not made up of a single group of people. It is made up of many peoples. Immigrants from Europe, Asia, Africa, and Central and South America settled in North America seeking a new life filled with opportunities unavailable in their homeland. Coming from many nations, they forged one nation and made it their own. More than 100 years ago, Walt Whitman expressed this perception of America as a melting pot: "Here is not merely a nation, but a teeming Nation of nations."

Although the ingenuity and acts of courage of these immigrants, our ancestors, shaped the North American way of life, we sometimes take their contributions for granted. This fine series, *The Peoples of North America,* examines the experiences and contributions of the immigrants and how these contributions determined the future of the United States and Canada.

Immigrants did not abandon their ethnic traditions when they reached the shores of North America. Each ethnic group had its own customs and traditions, and each brought different experiences, accomplishments, skills, values, styles of dress, and tastes in food that lingered long after its arrival. Yet this profusion of differences created a singularity, or bond, among the immigrants.

The United States and Canada are unusual in this respect. Whereas religious and ethnic differences have sparked intolerance throughout the rest of the world—from the 17th-century religious wars to the 19th-century nationalist movements in Europe to the near extermination of the Jewish people under Nazi Germany—North Americans have struggled to learn how to respect each other's differences and live in harmony.

Millions of immigrants from scores of homelands brought diversity to our continent. In a mass migration, some 12 million immigrants passed through the waiting rooms of New York's Ellis Island; thousands more came to the West Coast. At first, these immigrants were welcomed because labor was needed to meet the demands of the Industrial Age. Soon, however, the new immigrants faced the prejudice of earlier immigrants who saw them as a burden on the economy. Legislation was passed to limit immigration. The Chinese Exclusion Act of 1882 was among the first laws closing the doors to the promise of America. The Japanese were also effectively excluded by this law. In 1924, Congress set immigration quotas on a country-by-country basis.

Such prejudices might have triggered war, as they did in Europe, but North Americans chose negotiation and compromise, instead. This determination to resolve differences peacefully has been the hallmark of the peoples of North America.

The remarkable ability of Americans to live together as one people was seriously threatened by the issue of slavery. It was a symptom of growing intolerance in the world. Thousands of settlers from the British Isles had arrived in the colonies as indentured servants, agreeing to work for a specified number of years on farms or as apprentices in return for passage to America and room and board. When the first Africans arrived in the then-British colonies during the 17th century, some colonists thought that they too should be treated as indentured servants. Eventually, the question of whether the Africans should be viewed as indentured, like the English, or as slaves who could be owned for life, was considered in a Maryland court. The court's calamitous decree held that blacks were slaves bound to lifelong servitude, and so were their children.

America went through a time of moral examination and civil war before it finally freed African slaves and their descendants. The principle that all people are created equal had faced its greatest challenge and survived.

Yet the court ruling that set blacks apart from other races fanned flames of discrimination that burned long after slavery was abolished—and that still flicker today. The concept of racism had existed for centuries in countries throughout the world. For instance, when the Manchus conquered China in the 13th century, they decreed that Chinese and Manchus could not intermarry. To impress their superiority on the conquered Chinese, the Manchus ordered all Chinese men to wear their hair in a long braid called a queue.

By the 19th century, some intellectuals took up the banner of racism, citing Charles Darwin. Darwin's scientific studies hypothesized that highly evolved animals were dominant over other animals. Some advocates of this theory applied it to humans, asserting that certain races were more highly evolved than others and thus were superior.

This philosophy served as the basis for a new form of discrimination, not only against nonwhite people but also against various ethnic groups. Asians faced harsh discrimination and were depicted by popular 19th-century newspaper cartoonists as depraved, degenerate, and deficient in intelligence. When the Irish flooded American cities to escape the famine in Ireland, the cartoonists caricatured the typical "Paddy" (a common term for Irish immigrants) as an apelike creature with jutting jaw and sloping forehead.

By the 20th century, racism and ethnic prejudice had given rise to virulent theories of a Northern European master race. When Adolf Hitler came to power in Germany in 1933, he popularized the notion of Aryan supremacy. "Aryan," a term referring to the Indo-European races, was applied to so-called superior physical characteristics such as blond hair, blue eyes, and delicate facial features. Anyone with darker and heavier features was considered inferior. Buttressed by these theories, the German Nazi state from

1933 to 1945 set out to destroy European Jews, along with Poles, Russians, and other groups considered inferior. It nearly succeeded. Millions of these people were exterminated.

The tragedies brought on by ethnic and racial intolerance throughout the world demonstrate the importance of North America's efforts to create a society free of prejudice and inequality.

A relatively recent example of the New World's desire to resolve ethnic friction nonviolently is the solution the Canadians found to a conflict between two ethnic groups. A long-standing dispute as to whether Canadian culture was properly English or French resurfaced in the mid-1960s, dividing the peoples of the French-speaking Quebec Province from those of the English-speaking provinces. Relations grew tense, then bitter, then violent. The Royal Commission on Bilingualism and Biculturalism was established to study the growing crisis and to propose measures to ease the tensions. As a result of the commission's recommendations, all official documents and statements from the national government's capital at Ottawa are now issued in both French and English, and bilingual education is encouraged.

The year 1980 marked a coming of age for the United States's ethnic heritage. For the first time, the U.S. Census asked people about their ethnic background. Americans chose from more than 100 groups, including French Basque, Spanish Basque, French Canadian, Afro-American, Peruvian, Armenian, Chinese, and Japanese. The ethnic group with the largest response was English (49.6 million). More than 100 million Americans claimed ancestors from the British Isles, which includes England, Ireland, Wales, and Scotland. There were almost as many Germans (49.2 million) as English. The Irish-American population (40.2 million) was third, but the next largest ethnic group, the Afro-Americans, was a distant fourth (21 million). There was a sizable group of French ancestry (13 million), as well as of Italian (12 million). Poles, Dutch, Swedes, Norwegians, and Russians followed. These groups, and other smaller ones, represent the wondrous profusion of ethnic influences in North America.

Canada, too, has learned more about the diversity of its population. Studies conducted during the French/English conflict showed that Canadians were descended from Ukrainians, Germans, Italians, Chinese, Japanese, native Indians, and Eskimos, among others. Canada found it had no ethnic majority, although nearly half of its immigrant population had come from the British Isles. Canada, like the United States, is a land of immigrants for whom mutual tolerance is a matter of reason as well as principle.

The people of North America are the descendants of one of the greatest migrations in history. And that migration is not over. Koreans, Vietnamese, Nicaraguans, Cubans, and many others are heading for the shores of North America in large numbers. This mix of cultures shapes every aspect of our lives. To understand ourselves, we must know something about our diverse ethnic ancestry. Nothing so defines the North American nations as the motto on the Great Seal of the United States: *E Pluribus Unum*—Out of Many, One. ∾

In 1905 this immigrant couple exchanged vows in St. Mary's Romanian Orthodox Church in Cleveland, Ohio.

A WEDDING IN A NEW LAND

In an issue of *New Pioneer* magazine published in February 1943, Cornelia Porea recounts the marriage of her parents—John and Maria Porea—in Youngstown, Ohio. The wedding, which took place on August 5, 1905, was one of the first between Romanian immigrants in Youngstown's small Romanian colony. The 200-plus guests included other Americans curious to see a traditional, old-fashioned Romanian wedding.

The ceremony went smoothly, but the preparations for it had not. At the courthouse where John and Maria obtained the necessary legal papers, the American-born clerk had trouble spelling their last names. Then, the couple had been unable to find a priest of Romanian ancestry to perform the ceremony. At last John and Maria located a kindly Greek Orthodox priest willing to marry them. It was a concession but, after all, the couple planned to be married again in the old country— where the rest of their family and friends could see them.

At the reception, the guests feasted on *tocaina de gaina* (chicken stew) and *sarmale* (stuffed cabbage) and drank mugs of beer. Many in the party assembled on the floor and danced the *horas* and *serbas* to the accompaniment of clarinets and fiddles played by fellow immigrants. Then the *cinste* (wedding cash) was collected on small plates and counted.

Many Romanian immigrants became homesteaders in Canada's western provinces, such as Alberta, where these farmers posed for a photograph in 1928.

When the festivities ended, a Romanian immigrant stood up to give a speech. He told everyone that he had observed Maria since her arrival in America two years before and that she had shown great bravery, determination, and virtue in this new land. This guest added that the virtues of the bridegroom would also ensure the couple's success in America, and when they returned, wealthier and wiser, to their beloved Transylvania, they would bring wonderful memories of their experience in America.

These sentiments were shared by many Romanian immigrants at the turn of the 20th century, most of whom expected their stay in America to be temporary. A Romanian proverb—"Don't leave an old good friend of yours in order to please a new one"—summed up the immigrants' loyalty to their native land. Life in Romania had grown difficult, however, chiefly because of a shortage of arable land. Thus, in 1900–10, 53,000 Romanians came to America, followed by nearly 68,000 more in the next decade.

Many of the early immigrants hoped to earn enough money in the New World to buy land back in Romania. These newcomers had a motto: *mia si drumul* (roughly translated, "a thousand dollars and home again"). They left the exotic-sounding provinces of Transylvania, Bukovina, and the Banat, and hastened to New York, Chicago, Philadelphia, Detroit, Cleveland, Pittsburgh, and smaller cities, such as Youngstown. A smaller number of Romanian immigrants went to Canada. There they settled not in cities but in rural areas where 160 acres of land awaited any pioneer willing to cultivate the land and pay a yearly tax on it of $10.

Most Romanians who immigrated to North America were originally farmers. These newcomers eluded exact identification, however, largely because Romania's population included so many diverse elements. Between 1881 and 1900 the Bureau of Immigration listed the majority of Romanian immigrants as Jews. By 1929 some 50,000 Romanian Jews had landed on American shores. The 150,000 other Romanian immigrants included Hungarians, Germans, Armenians, and Gypsies. These groups seldom mixed in North America, and the approximately 315,000 Romanian Americans listed in the 1980 Census remain a many-faceted group.

After World War II, yet another group of Romanians began entering North America—intellectuals and dissidents anxious to escape a Romanian government that functioned as a satellite of the Soviet Union. These political refugees have sometimes felt at odds with previous generations of immigrants and their offspring. Kenneth Thigpen, in his book *Folklore and the Ethnicity Factor in the Lives of Romanian Americans*, asserts that the more established Romanian Americans distrust the younger, more educated and worldly immigrants. The conflict between these groups is one of many that makes the story of Romanian Americans distinctive and fascinating. ∾

THE ROMANIANS IN THEIR HOMELAND

The ancestors of modern-day Romanians were the Dacians, a people whom the ancient Greek historian Herodotus characterized in the 5th century B.C. as "very brave and honest fighters." They inhabited an area in southeastern Europe where they farmed, bred cattle, and mined gold and silver. By the 2nd century B.C. this mineral wealth had enabled the Dacians to carry on lively trading partnerships and to expand their borders. By the 1st century A.D. the leaders of the vast Roman Empire were so alarmed by the Dacians' advances that they engaged them in battle.

Rome's superior forces prevailed, and in A.D. 129 the emperor Hadrian divided Dacia into two provinces. His successor, Marcus Aurelius, divided it further. By this time, Dacia covered a region roughly the site of present-day Romania. Colonists arrived from Rome, mingling with the native population, and the Romans dubbed the country *Roma* (Rome) *Nea* (New), hence, eventually, Romania (spellings also used are Rumania and Roumania). In the 3rd century, the Romans withdrew, pressured by the Goths, a tribe that invaded from the east.

Two important Roman legacies lingered. The first, Christianity, came to Romania through the efforts of missionaries shortly after the conversion of the Roman emperor Constantine in the year 312. The second leg-

acy, Latin, became the basis of the Romanian tongue still spoken today. Because of its Roman origins, Romanian qualifies as a Romance language, like French, Italian, and Spanish. In fact, Romanian is the only Romance language that developed in the eastern part of Latin (Roman) Europe.

The Chain of Invasions

The Romanian language, though based on Latin, includes a mosaic of influences that provide an index to the country's many invaders. The Goths gave way to the Huns, the Slavs, and others. A steadying influence appeared in the country in the 7th century, when Bulgars arrived from the south and ruled for 200 years. Under their dominion, Romania switched its religious allegiance from Roman Catholicism to a rival branch of Christianity, Eastern Orthodoxy, following the conversion of Bulgaria's czar Boris in 864. Yet another invasion occurred at the end of the 9th century. Magyars from Hungary—which lies off Romania's northwestern border—drove out the Bulgars. The Magyars, in turn, bowed before the Mongols, an Asiatic people, in 1241. Some historians claim that this chain of invasions destroyed the original Daco-Roman population; others argue that its remnants escaped into the Carpathian Mountains—a northeastern range near the Russian border—and that these survivors are the ancestors of today's Romanians.

Either way, the Mongol occupation ended in the

This gold helmet, unearthed in Romania, dates from the 5th century B.C., when the Dacians earned a reputation as "brave and honest fighters."

Bran Castle, built in 1377–78, defended the road linking Transylvania with Walachia in the era of Turkish invasions.

13th century, and two independent Romanian nations emerged south of the Carpathian Mountains: Walachia and Moldavia. Both were feudal principalities, that is, states ruled by a *voivode* (prince) in an agrarian economy supported by a caste of *boyars*—landowners—who themselves ruled over a large population of sharecroppers. These sharecroppers, or serfs, comprised the bulk of the population but were forced to turn over most of their harvests to the boyars.

This system stayed in place for centuries, even as further invasions occurred. In the 14th century, the Turkish (Ottoman) Empire advanced into central Europe, and the Turks mounted a series of sieges against Walachia and Moldavia. At first the principalities managed to stave off attack, but eventually they succumbed—Walachia in 1417 and Moldavia in 1541.

Native Romanians nominally held governing posts, but they answered to the Turkish government until the early 18th century, when two other powers, Austria and Russia, flexed their imperial muscles.

Eager to cast off the Turkish yoke, Romanian leaders in Walachia and Moldavia secretly plotted with Austria and Russia. The Turks, alerted to this intrigue, hit upon a new way of keeping the Romanians in line. They dispatched into the principalities a ruling class of Phanariots—Greeks from Constantinople (present-day Istanbul). The repressive Phanariot regime lasted until 1821, though individual leaders, or *hospidars*, lasted only a year or two before giving way to replacements shuttled into office by the Turkish government.

This engraving depicts Ottoman Turks storming Constantinople in the 15th century. Later, the Turks dispatched Phanariots— members of the city's Greek population—to rule Romania's rebellious principalities.

Meanwhile, Russia commenced hostilities with the Turks, driving them out of the principalities in 1769. This conflict ended in 1774, and a peace treaty ceded Walachia and Moldavia back to Turkey, with the provision that the Romanians be treated fairly. Turkey agreed to the arrangement but immediately violated it, leading to resumed skirmishes with Russia that lasted until 1792, when a new treaty was signed, again conferring privileges on Walachia and Moldavia. Once more, however, the Ottoman Turks ignored the pact and continued their revolving-door approach to government, rotating hospidars almost yearly. Finally, in 1802, Russia intervened, decreeing that each ruler stay in place for seven years.

In 1806 Turkey, egged on by an emissary of the French emperor Napoleon, removed Romania's hospidars without the approval of Russia, which reacted by sending its own forces into the principalities. The next six years proved disastrous for Romania, as Russia bled its economy—carrying off its produce, debasing its coinage, and exiling protesters to distant Siberia. In 1812, Russia went a step further, attempting to incorporate the principalities into its own empire; it managed to secure southern Moravia, or Bessarabia.

Conflict raged on. In 1821, a Phanariot leader, Ypsilanti, tried to claim Moldavia and Walachia for his ancestral nation, Greece. The Turks expelled the Phanariots, aided by the Romanians, whom the Phanariots had previously mistreated. The next year Turkey let Romanian nationals rule the principalities; they received lifelong appointments after another war between Turkey and Russia, in 1828–29. From this point on, though Walachia and Moldavia officially belonged to the Ottoman Empire, they fell under the protection of Russia, which, for once, actually aided the principalities. It modernized the country by building roads, convening an assembly that drew up a constitution, introducing factories, and encouraging active foreign trade.

With progress came the desire for independence, which culminated in the revolution of 1848–49. The Russians suppressed the Romanians, helped by Turkey, but withdrew in 1854, weakened by their defeat in the Crimean War (waged against a powerful alliance formed by Great Britain, France, Turkey, and Sardinia). Romania came under the neutral guardianship of Austria. In 1856, the Treaty of Paris designated Walachia and Moldavia as principalities, again under Turkish rule—though supervised by the European powers—and restored Bessarabia to Moldavia.

In 1859 the efforts of young Romanian nationalists led to the establishment of the autonomous United Principalities, known as Romania. A nobleman, Prince Alexandru Cuza, occupied the throne and tried to introduce democracy overnight by instating a constitution, granting all citizens the right to vote, and emancipating the peasants from their servitude to the boyars. The boyars became enraged and forced Cuza to abdicate in 1866. Eleven years later, his replacement, Carol I, a German, led Romania into war on the side of Russia

Russia withdrew from Moldavia and Walachia in 1854, during the Crimean War. Much of the conflict took place in southwestern Russia, where this encampment was photographed.

In 1859 Prince Alexandru Cuza became the first leader of the United Principalities—or Romania.

and against Turkey. In 1878, Russia prevailed, and at the Congress of Berlin, the European powers affirmed Romania's independence.

The Modern Era

Romania, free at last, bore the deep scars of almost continual invasion, and its inhabitants had yet to cohere into a unified people. Unlike some European nations, Romania had only slowly begun to develop a workable and fair system of government. Prince Carol tried to guide the country toward stability, but without success, as one government after another collapsed. Finally, however, a firm ruler emerged, the legislative leader Ion Bratianu, who became premier in 1876 and held power as a virtual dictator for the next dozen years.

Bratianu headed Romania's Liberal party, which favored strengthening the middle, commercial class. As a result, Romania's overall economy improved, subsidized by foreign capital that fostered the growth of industries, railroads, and institutions. The gains achieved by the middle class piqued struggling peasants. In 1864

Romania's Iron Guard, an anti-Semitic group from Moldavia, marched through Bucharest on November 8, 1936.

In 1938 Romania's king Carol II ceded lands to Germany and Russia—uneasy allies that had signed a short-lived nonaggression pact. Later, Carol visited Romanian soldiers who fought beside the Nazis in World War II.

they had won emancipation from serfdom, which had bound them to the boyars' land, but the problem of poverty went unsolved as many poor farmers grew indebted to moneylenders. Tensions mounted, and in 1907 the peasants staged a revolt, driving the governing regime from office.

Since the Congress of Berlin, Romania had managed to avoid armed conflict with its neighbors. The Balkan Wars of 1912–13 upset the calm. Romania gained southern Dobruja, on the Bulgarian border, after besting that neighbor. Then World War I began. Romania declared itself neutral, but joined the Allies in 1916 against the Austro-German powers, who responded by overrunning the country. The Allies prevailed in 1918, and Romania prospered in postwar negotiations, regaining Bessarabia and annexing land from Austria and Hungary.

Internally, Romania's problems mounted as inequities persisted between the nation's classes. In 1914, the country's population had totaled 7.6 million—excluding Transylvania and Bessarabia, which lay in foreign hands. Peasants composed 75 percent of this total, yet they lacked a voice in their nation's policies, a fact cruelly driven home in 1926, when revamped electoral laws locked opposition parties out of power.

Soon, however, matters changed. Romania's monarch, King Ferdinand, died, and so did the legislative mogul, Bratianu. Their deaths cleared the way for the National Peasant Party, which in 1928 won 75 percent of the vote. Headed by Iuliu Maniu, this populist party dismantled the oppressive apparatus of the previous regime, abolishing censorship, diminishing police power, and granting greater freedom to Transylvania. The party also encouraged peasants to form cooperative farming ventures. However, in 1930 difficulties arose once more. Maniu invited Carol II to assume the kingship, but friction developed between the two leaders—in part because Carol broke his vow to reconcile with his wife, Queen Helen, and to terminate his liaison with his mistress. At the same time the world economic crisis ruined the policies of the peasants' party, which fell from power. In addition, Carol sought to weaken other sources of opposition and did so with the help of an emerging cadre of Moldavian fascists known as the Iron Guard.

The Iron Guard catered to Romanian anti-Semitic sentiment that dated back to the days when poor farmers had racked up staggering debts to Jewish moneylenders; in fact, the 1907 uprising had been directed mainly against Jews. Also, when the Iron Guard entered the stage, they could point to the examples of Germany and Italy as nations prospering under fascist rule. Indeed, in 1937 King Carol accepted a trade treaty with Nazi Germany. At this point the Iron Guard and an equally reactionary group, the National Christian Party, raised anti-Semitic prejudices to a dangerous pitch and dragged the entire nation toward tyranny.

In an attempt to subdue the fascists, who had taken control of the government, Carol dissolved the parliament in 1938 and proclaimed a royal dictatorship. A

After World War II, Romania became a satellite of the Soviet Union, which instituted farming collectives such as this one in Moldavia.

year later, at the outset of World War II, Romania ceded some of its acquired provinces in order to appease Russia and Germany, which had signed a short-lived nonaggression pact. Faced by these losses, Carol abdicated in 1940, and his son Michael took the throne. The real power behind the government, however, was General Ion Antonescu, who created a new cabinet, appointed himself Romania's actual leader, and announced an alliance with Nazi Germany.

World War II concluded in 1945 with Germany's defeat; Romania fell with it. Three years later, the Soviet Union installed a Communist dictatorship that answered to the dictator in Moscow, Joseph Stalin. Romanian Stalinists formulated an economic plan that included running farms along the rigidly controlled lines practiced in Russia. Stalin died in 1953, replaced by the moderate Nikita Khrushchev, and tensions eased between Russia and the West. Romania seized this opportunity to assert its right to follow its own "road to socialism." In 1964, the country formally declared its independence from the Soviets. Since 1967, when General Secretary Nicolae Ceauşescu became head of state, the country has faced the difficult task of trying to better the lot of the people through economic development while keeping an eye on the reactions of the Kremlin.

At almost any time in Romania's long, painful history, its citizens had ample reason to flee their troubled land. Few did, however, until the late 19th century.

In the early 1900s Cleveland became home to many Romanian immigrants, such as the Farcasius, who posed in native garb for this photograph.

LEAVING HOME

In his memoir *An American in the Making*, M. E. Ravage recalls the final moments leading up to his departure from a small Romanian town, on his way to the New World:

> What did one do? Perhaps the best thing to do was not to think of the present, but to concentrate on the past and the future. There are messages from everyone to be delivered to relatives in the new land. Shake hands with the people of the community—many of whom were strangers up until this moment.

Everyone at the train station seemed calm, Ravage writes, until the engine chugged into view, then suddenly some people broke into tears. A young boy at the time, Ravage was surprised when his mother embraced him violently, with "a despair . . . which I could not then understand." In time, however, understanding came to him, as it did to his fellow immigrants.

Where Did They Come From?

Between 1870 and 1900, some 18,000 American immigrants listed Romania as their country of origin. Before 1895, most were Jews from Moldavia, Russian-controlled Bessarabia, or Austrian-held Bukovina. Thereafter, the majority of newcomers consisted of peasants from Transylvania. Others hailed from Macedonia (a mountainous region divided today among

This immigrant ship landed in Boston in about 1920. The cost of a transatlantic ticket bankrupted many Romanian passengers.

Greece, Yugoslavia, and Bulgaria), Turkey, northern Greece, and Albania. (Macedonian Romanians spoke a distinct dialect based on Romanian but containing elements borrowed from Greek and Albanian.)

By 1920, more than 85 percent of the 85,000 Romanian immigrants in the United States came from Transylvania, Bukovina, or the Banat, territories annexed by the Romanian kingdom in 1918. The advent of these newcomers, whose ancestry was not strictly Romanian, makes it difficult to determine the precise number of Romanian Americans. Similarly, Romanians from Dobruja may have been counted as Turks or Bulgarians by immigration officials.

Most of these immigrants had been struggling, independent farmers in their native land. After the 1864 law abolishing serfdom many families acquired stable land holdings, but an inheritance law soon went into effect, stipulating that land be divided equally among all the children in a family. As a result, a large number of Romanians came into possession of parcels of land so small that their owners faced perpetual debt. Peasants could borrow money at low rates, and government legislation—passed by the assembly in 1871, 1899, and 1902—offered assistance. Still, peasants felt frozen on the lowest rung of Romania's economic ladder.

Another cause of emigration from Romania emerged in 1867, when the "Dual Monarchy"—a pact between Romania and Hungary—made Transylvania answerable to the central Hungarian government in Budapest. This government instituted a program of "Magyarization" that impinged on the freedom of Transylvanians in schools, in civil service, and in society. The Hungarian leaders also tried to convert their new subjects to Roman Catholicism; the Transylvanians, mostly members of the Eastern Orthodox church, grew more and more frustrated, not only with Budapest but with the central Romanian government in Bucharest.

Their frustration extended even to Romania's constitution, as the scholar Christine Galitzi explains in her 1929 study of Romanian Americans. According to Galitzi, the amended Constitution of 1884 divided the Romanian population into three classes of electors, whose power corresponded to their income. Thus, even though the peasants composed Romania's majority, they belonged to the third—or lowest—electoral class and had less say than their wealthier compatriots.

Still another obstacle barred the peasants from gaining a voice: Many were illiterate and thus unable to communicate on the large scale necessary to achieve unity as a political group. All Romanians could learn to read and write in public schools—in fact, the country had a policy of compulsory education reinforced with fines for noncompliance. But peasants often preferred to pay the fine rather than give up a pair of arms needed to help with farmwork. "Born a peasant, always a peasant" was a popular saying.

Disease and filth caused many deaths during the long voyage, particularly among children, a sad fact dramatized in this newspaper illustration published in 1882.

Taking the Risk

At the turn of the 20th century the fare for passage to New York was 200 francs, so high a price that a household often had to hock all its belongings simply to finance one immigrant. And the cost was astronomical for those who brought along entire families, which in Romania typically included five children and sometimes grandparents, aunts, and cousins. Money also had to cover other necessary items such as passports and changes of clothing.

Romanians who dithered about risking so much looked to the example of kin who had already braved the journey. Many of these pioneers sent back encouraging news, but some reports sounded a disheartening note. In addition, Romanians often found it difficult to stay in contact with immigrants—an inquiring letter mailed from Bucharest to a relative in the New World might receive no response because the immigrant had moved to a new address. Many Romanians began to believe that those who succeeded in America had become selfish and wanted to keep the promised land entirely to themselves. To cap off these doubts, Romanian immigrants faced the trauma of leaving behind a known world for one they could only guess at. Ravage eloquently sums up the immigrant's dilemma:

> Well, try to think of leavetaking—of farewells to home and kindred, in all likelihood never to be seen again; of last looks lingering affectionately on things and places; of ties broken and grown stronger in the breaking. Try to think of the deep upheaval of the human soul, pulled up by the roots from its ancient, precious soil, cast abroad among you here, withering for a space, then slowly finding nourishment in the new soil, and once more thriving—not, indeed, as before—a novel, composite growth. If you can see this you may form some idea of the sadness and glory of his adventure.

The immigrant center at Ellis Island opened in 1892, processing millions of immigrants, such as those shown in this 1906 photograph.

The Journey

Today European immigrants travel from their home to the airport and less than ten hours later pass through customs at an American airport. The fare can prove expensive, but the trip itself involves little hardship. In the early 20th century, circumstances were much different. Romanian immigrants first had to reach a port, often journeying from small, out-of-the-way towns, then proceed up the Danube River toward Hamburg, Germany. From there they boarded ships that made the transatlantic voyage. The following stories, recorded in I. L. Popescu's *Land of Promise*, describe the experience of a few Romanians headed for Canada.

Mrs. Dominica Lupastean eventually wound up in Regina, Saskatchewan, a province in western Canada. As the family prepared to leave in 1912, one member expressed skepticism:

> "I don't go," said mother. "I prefer my poverty to a foreign land." Father had a passport for the whole family. God, he had bought tickets for the Titanic. Seeing that he couldn't convince Mother, he sold the tickets and bought just one ticket for another ship. Mother was everybody's luck! In the end, she agreed to go on, urged by her brother, Ion: "Dominica, you mustn't make the mistake not to follow your man. . . . You know, on top of it all, you're pregnant. . . ." She was pregnant with my brother Nick. So, she shared the cattle between the relatives and, eyes full of tears, we left all one morning for Hamburg. There was a cattle boat waiting for us there which, anyway, didn't collide with any iceberg as the Titanic did.

During the voyage, sudden illness often turned into tragedy because doctors and nurses were in short supply. Tilly Lipan, also of Regina, recalled:

> We boarded at Tulcea an old little steamer. She was sailing with difficulty along the Danube . . . where the

water was not deep and the sailors kept prodding the bottom, plunging some poles now and then into the water. We were a family of seven. . . . My sister Ileana was two. She kept crying almost all the time. . . . Ileana had a sore belly, she had got dysentery. And there was no doctor or medicine on the ship . . . we found her dead one morning. . . . Mother wanted a decent burial in a graveyard . . . five days before reaching Halifax the captain ordered our Ileana thrown

Immigrants sometimes waited for weeks at Ellis Island, taking their meals in the center's large dining hall, a portion of which appears in this 1907 photograph.

over board right away. He wouldn't listen to Mother's and Father's begging and to our crying; that captain said he was not authorized to carry corpses as an epidemic might start. Poor Ileana was the toll taken by my father's land-hunger.

A third immigrant, Leona Muntean, who sailed with her family from Hamburg to Halifax, Canada, remembered the cruel behavior of the shipping line's employees: "The agents were shouting so loud that all the children were frightened. . . . They were holding bayonets, one meter long. To cut the baggage with. They cut all our luggage . . . they took whatever they liked." Once the ship set sail, Leona Muntean and her siblings ventured on deck, repeatedly asking their father to point out America. " 'Over there,' " would answer Father, showing a chance direction with his hand . . . And we would wait in vain for hours on end to catch a

This 1921 cartoon typifies the antiforeign sentiment common in America after World War I. In 1921 the U.S. Congress established the first national quota system, limiting immigration on a nation-by-nation basis.

sight of America. . . . Only after 16 days did we see something . . . . First, I thought it was a cloud. . . . Then, just another, larger ship. . . . " 'Look, Father, a big ship!' " " 'That's no ship,' " he said, looking in that direction. " 'That's Halifax.' "

Getting In

The first glimpse of Canada Romanian immigrants had was the port city of Halifax; those landing in the United States entered New York Harbor. They sighted the Statue of Liberty, then Castle Garden, an old fortress converted into an immigration center in 1885. In 1892 it was replaced by Ellis Island, which was built on the site of an old naval arsenal. Ellis Island remained the gateway to America until 1932, when it became a detention center. Closed in 1954, Ellis Island sat unused for more than a decade, and in 1965, the federal government refurbished it and opened it to the public as a museum commemorating the millions of immigrants who passed through it.

At Ellis Island newcomers received an efficient but impersonal welcome. After quarantine and customs procedures, the immigrants submitted to health inspections. Several doctors—each on the lookout for signs of a specific disease—sped through the crowd. A "matron" examined pregnant women, and specialists stood by to solve doubtful or puzzling cases. Immigrants who survived this initial screening were grilled by clerks—almost none of whom spoke Romanian—who jotted down notes for a detailed report on all the applicants, including their reasons for immigrating, their acquaintances or kin in the New World, and the amount of cash in their possession. Exhausted, bewildered, and frightened, immigrants next proceeded to a special office where they could exchange currency, purchase rail tickets, and send telegrams to friends or kin living in North America.

Such was the experience of those Romanians who successfully entered America. Many others, however,

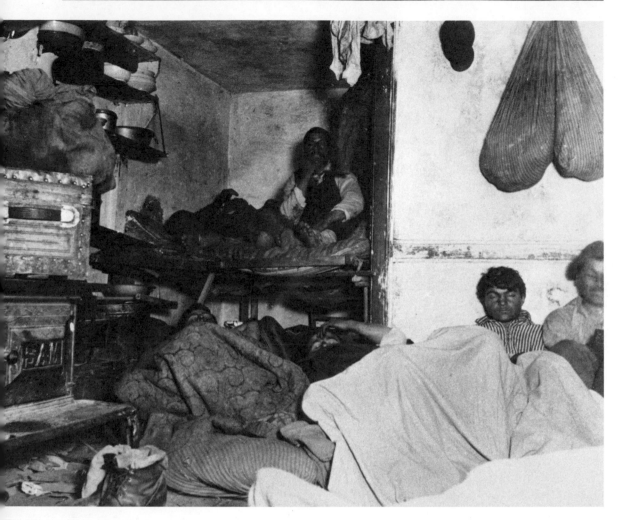

*Most Romanian immigrants
began their American experience
in New York City, where they
huddled in overcrowded and
unsanitary tenements.*

never made it, barred by quotas. Between 1882 and 1929 Congress enacted several major laws designed to prevent "undesirables" from emigrating to America. First came the Chinese Exclusion Act, a response to American workers threatened by competition from cheap Asian labor. That same year another law singled out Slavs, Magyars, Jews, Sicilians, and Romanians. This legislation reflected the growing sentiment among some established Americans that immigrants from southern and eastern Europe belonged to inferior racial stock and would either pollute the existing population or utterly fail to mix with it.

This second measure allowed for the deportation of "undesirables" who had slipped through the cracks and entered the country. Steamship companies were ordered to return to their homelands all passengers deemed unhealthy, especially those with so-called loathsome diseases, such as typhoid, typhus, and cholera. A third measure excluded polygamists (though multiple wives were allowed to such natives as the Mormons). In 1917 this bill was supplemented with a literacy test that furnished authorities with yet another excuse for rejecting applicants.

The first actual quota law appeared in 1924 and went into effect five years later. Its "national origins" provision limited the number of European immigrants to 150,000 per year, apportioning them on a nation-by-nation basis. The more immigrants who had already arrived from a given country, the more could follow. Thus hopefuls from northern and western Europe received favorable treatment, at the expense of those from the east and south, such as Romanians.

The quota system, patently racist, suffered from inefficiency. Foreign countries had a hard time fitting citizens into the crude classifications designed by American immigration authorities. Romania, for example, included people of various descent: Bulgarians, Hungarians, Turks, Jews, Gypsies, and others. Which among them counted as "true" Romanians? A similar difficulty existed in Germany, Czechoslovakia, and Yugoslavia. Then there was the matter of borders: Poland's boundaries expanded and contracted, and Austrian, Russian, German, and Baltic nationals sometimes qualified for admission under the quota system, and sometimes did not. These difficulties, along with the resumption of a friendlier immigration policy, helped abolish quota systems after World War II.

First Days in New York

Once Romanian immigrants survived the dilemma of leaving, the ordeal of the voyage, and the indignities of Ellis Island, the drama of resettlement awaited them. Before embarking for distant cities where kin and work could be found, newcomers usually stayed for a short while in New York City, trying to acclimate themselves to the New World. Imagine the shock of the rural Romanian immigrant, walking the streets of New York City, assaulted on all sides by new laws, customs, and a new language, not to mention the frightening pace of urban life.

Few of New York City's Romanian immigrants ventured into handsome Manhattan neighborhoods unless summoned there to perform menial tasks such as clearing snow from the streets.

Quickly, Romanian immigrants noticed that the vast city contained a patchwork of distinct neighborhoods, many of them housing different ethnic populations. Jews and Italians often lived downtown, Germans on the Upper East Side, and Romanians in the West 60s. Most new arrivals gravitated toward neighborhoods inhabited by their compatriots, and these neighborhoods flourished as self-contained miniatures of the homeland. Here immigrants discovered lodging and kinship and also took the measure of the changes wrought by America on previous arrivals. Soon after M. E. Ravage arrived, he met a Romanian American whose success had weakened his bond with the old country and imbued him with a cynical outlook. The man's wife, Ravage wrote, "intimated that in America there were no such things as relatives; that money was a man's best friend, and that the wisest course was to depend on oneself."

Newcomers sometimes cringed to see respectable, established people from their village hawking newspapers, soda water, or pickles. Ravage, for example, was distressed at his cousin Betty's lack of shame as she sauntered "airily" amid New York City's urban squalor. He wrote, "I asked myself whether I, too, would harden and forget the better days I had known, and I fervently hoped not." ∾

Like many male Romanian immigrants, this Cleveland group roomed in a boardinghouse near their place of employment.

SETTLING IN

In a 1978 issue of the *American Roumanian Review*, an article appeared, written by Theodor Andrica, a Romanian American, in which the author reminisced about his family's move to a comfortable, middle-class neighborhood in Cleveland, Ohio, just before World War II. At the time, Andrica's mother was expected to arrive from the old country, and his many preparations for her visit included purchasing a new Oriental rug to cover the parquet floor in his apartment.

During the first few days of her stay, Mrs. Andrica seemed very content, and her son's success in America clearly impressed her. But then she learned that he rented rather than owned his apartment. After criticizing him severely, she grew silent, refusing to talk to him for days. When at last she spoke, she reminded him that in Romania even the itinerant Gypsies paid rent to no one. How could Theodor Andrica consider himself a "success"?

Andrica immediately got in touch with a realtor and begged him to find a modest house. "Remember," his mother warned, "I don't want any barracks or somebody's discarded house." When a suitable place turned up she demanded a photograph of it to send to her friends back home. Thereafter, Andrica noted, "my mother was a changed woman. She kept polishing the floors, washing the windows, whether it was needed or

Before immigrating, most Romanians, such as these Jews outside the city of Iasi, struggled to farm small plots of land.

not." In her letters to her friends she told them how she didn't have to split wood anymore and how the house's heat could be regulated by a fixture on the wall that one did not even have to light with a match.

Urban living obviously pleased Mrs. Andrica. She proudly referred to her son as a "successful American." He had moved from a farm in Romania to a city in America and now owned his own piece of the new land. Some aspects of ownership puzzled her, however—the water bill, for one. "Water comes from God," she said. "Who pays God for the water?"

On the Move

Romanian immigrants tended to settle in the industrialized areas of the mid-Atlantic and Great Lakes states, congregating in urban centers such as New York, Philadelphia, Detroit, Chicago, Pittsburgh, and Cleveland, and in smaller cities such as Youngstown, Canton, and Akron, Ohio; Homestead, Erie, New Castle, and Scalp Level, Pennsylvania; and East Chicago and Gary, Indiana. Smaller numbers headed west to Minnesota, Missouri, and Montana.

As a rule Romanian immigrants avoided farm work. Christine Galitzi's study of Romanian assimilation cites three reasons for this phenomenon. First, in the port cities where new arrivals landed, agents looking for cheap labor awaited them and lured them into factories, going so far as to arrange transportation and lodging for the "greenhorns," or newcomers. Second, industrial jobs paid more reliably than did farming, and immi-

As a rule Romanian men avoided farmwork, favoring the regular wages they could obtain in other forms of labor. These immigrants found jobs in Pittsburgh's coal mines.

Detroit's car manufacturers employed Romanian immigrants on their assembly lines.

grants liked being able to measure their progress immediately in dollars and cents. Finally, Romanian immigrants, who often traveled in groups, feared being split up, a likelier prospect on farms, which had fewer openings for laborers at any given time. In the city, immigrants could live and work together. Consider the story of Mr. B., excerpted from Galitzi's study:

When eleven of us landed in New York in 1902, we met an agent right at the steamer's gang-plank. He spoke Romanian mixed with a few words of German. He offered to employ us at $9 a week at the Baltimore and Ohio Railroad Company in Garrett, Indiana. He assured us that we would have our wages paid regularly every week and in case we were willing to go to Garrett he would put us on the train and have us met at the place of our destination. With such offers he seemed like a God-send to us. None of us spoke English. . . . We had no idea as to the kind of work we might get

(continued on page 57)

A NEW COMMUNITY

Overleaf: *Émigré photographer Alfred Kaufmann offers a unique glimpse of New York City's Romanian-American community.*

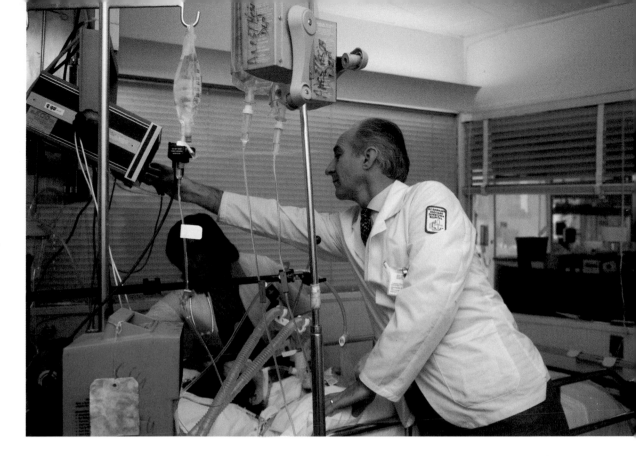

The Stratomirs fled Romania's Soviet regime and now live in Jackson Heights, an ethnic neighborhood in the borough of Queens. Upper left: *The family relaxes in a local park.* Far left: *Tatania Stratomir's English-language lessons helped her land a drafting job with an architectural firm.* Above: *George Stratomir, who holds a Romanian medical degree, works in a laboratory at the Beekman Downtown Hospital in Manhattan.* Left: *Ann Marie Stratomir does homework in the family's apartment.*

The Nitzas own a thriving bakery in Sunnyside, Queens. Here they put the finishing touches on Romanian delicacies. Back from the office, Tatania Stratomir fixes dinner while her husband looks on. At Transylvania, a favorite restaurant in Sunnyside, diners feast beneath a portrait of Count Dracula, the legendary Romanian vampire often featured in fiction and film.

The noi-veniti *labor at many different occupations.* Facing page: *An artist poses in his Queens studio.* Above: *A realtor places a "sold" sign on property that has just been bought.* Below: *Ilie Dumitru operates a hot dog stand near midtown Manhattan.*

Like many other immigrants, those from Romania often drive taxis. This cabbie poses below the Brooklyn Bridge.

(continued from page 48)

. . . . as the agent was willing to engage us at once we
accepted his offer in order not to break our group
and so we all went to Garrett, where we found immediate
employment.

Immigrants commonly found jobs in iron and steel
factories, in coal mining and meat packing, and in the
automobile and rubber industries. They worked as
stokers, molders, smelters, iron casters, miners, and so
on, until they developed sufficient command of English
to advance into supervisory positions. Women worked,
too. Most entered the clothing, or garment, business,
and some found employment in the cigar and tobacco
industries and in slaughterhouses. Relatively few
sought domestic posts as maids or washerwomen, dis-
couraged in part by the language barrier.

Immigrant men who journeyed alone to America
usually led a transitory existence, remaining a year or
two in the first city where they found employment, then
moving on to another city where friends or relatives
secured work for them. Sometimes they settled per-
manently in this second place, but more often they tried
out two or three more cities before ending their migration. Free to test the New World, they continually
sought to better their circumstances.

Boardinghouses

Single men preferred the convenience of living near the
factory where they worked, sometimes on the same
street. Boardinghouses had rooms to let, and Romanian
immigrants generally found lodgings alongside their
compatriots. Some boardinghouses rented all their
space to immigrants who all came from the same Romanian village. Boardinghouses thus served as community centers. Gerald Bobango's *Romanian Orthodoxy
in Youngstown, 1906–1981* includes an interview with
Nick Tecau, a Romanian who immigrated to America

in the early 20th century. Asked why he chanced a new start in the United States, Tecau responded:

> Well, I had a brother here—in Ilasco, Missouri, about one mile from Hannibal. There was a lot of Romanians there, and two-three boarding houses. Now let me tell you what we ate there . . . a pretty good lunch we had, and there were 18–20 men in one house made of birch logs, like a barracks.
> Q. How much did you pay for boarding?
> A. I come to that. For supper, we had pretty much the same thing. Soup, fried meat, pastry, you know. Now you guess how much a month we paid for board and washing.
> Q. Ten—let's see, about seven or eight dollars?
> A. You heard about it, huh?

The Romanians in America, by Vladimir Wertsman, contains an article written by an early immigrant and published in a popular Romanian-American periodical. It vividly conveys what life was like for men living together in boardinghouses. Usually these residences had two stories. The downstairs consisted of a large kitchen, dining room, and parlor. Upstairs were seven or eight bedrooms and a couple of bathrooms. These accommodated 25–30 boarders, though as many as 60 squeezed into some establishments. All the boarders knew one another and identified themselves not only by name but by their village of origin.

Although numerous ties bound the boarders, they fell into two distinct groups: the "foreboarders," who paid $8–12 for lodging, laundry, and food; and the "community" boarders, who paid the landlord's wife $3 per month for bedding, washing, and cooking, with the cost of the food divided among the "company." In addition to serving supper, boardinghouse keepers provided lunches that their tenants ate on the job. These lunches, prepared the previous evening, included sandwiches, sausages or pork chops, two eggs, a piece of fruit, a pickle, and lots of fresh black coffee brewed the same morning.

In the evening, the boarders dined in a large room, sitting on benches pulled up to a long table. The meal customarily began with the oldest man present reciting the Lord's Prayer. Each month the diners received a special treat: a four-gallon keg of beer. Failure to provide this gift—or *cinste*—could cost a landlord his or her business. After supper, the men gathered to drink beer and one of the company might pull out a wooden flute, providing accompaniment for the others as they

This photograph, taken in about 1910, shows homes built for workers by a Pittsburgh mining company.

In Canada opportunities awaited immigrants willing to clear and farm the country's unsettled western provinces. Here, a Romanian Canadian operates a horse-drawn wheat thresher.

sang the *doine*, a melancholy tune. Improvised lyrics expressed the men's sadness and regret at being so far away from their homeland and loved ones. The evening concluded with the boarders retiring to their rooms. Under each immigrant's bed sat a wooden box that held his belongings, including money—few Romanians trusted banks. After looking through their goods, the men slept, gaining strength for the morning, when they arose early and trudged off to the factory.

The Homesteading Romanian Canadians

The experience of the Romanians who ventured to Canada differed from that of those who settled in urban America. In Canada, Romanian immigrants had a chance to procure homesteads, generally in the western provinces, and thus bypassed the urban life for the wild and wide-open spaces. Here is the story of Gheorghe Costron, from Regina, Saskatchewan, as recorded in I. L. Popescu's book *Land of Promise*:

> I had come to this country hoping to make some money and go back. But the agents would pester me: "Get

yourself a homestead! Get yourself a homestead! . . .
So's you can live free . . ." So, I couldn't go back.
I got a homestead near Rouleau. I traveled by train
from Regina to Rouleau. From there, southwards,
another 40 miles I walked. . . . And then, go and
search . . . Boy, boy . . . and a stranger was I . . . I
was like a calf astray from his mother . . walking like a
man lost in the desert . . . the suffering that one
brings to oneself . . . In time I started to work, I got
used to everything. Living now here and then there
. . . . In the spring I bought lumber and returned to
my land to build a tiny little shack and a stable . . . .
And everything followed.

*The Albina Foreign Exchange
in Youngstown, Ohio, changed
American dollars into
Romanian currency for
immigrants who returned to the
old country.*

The lure of money impelled even well-off Romanians to travel across the sea and brave the unrelenting
elements of Western Canada. In *Land of Promise*, Maria

Rosca tells what happened to her father during a terrible storm one Christmas night:

> When father, Constantin Dragu, left Hirsova, he didn't
> want to sell his land; he leased on a five-year term 30
> acres and the garden by the house . . . He said he was
> going to stay 3-4 years in Canada and then come back.
> For, my mother-in-law too, said: 'Why should he go
> and live among strangers when he has so much land?'
> . . . To die in the prairie, may God rest his soul . . .
> He froze dead, poor him, right in the second year
> of life on the homestead.

The reminiscences of the Romanians in Canada are filled with toil and tragedy, yet the pioneers stayed. Some, worn down by the harsh winters, longed to go back. Ilie Lupastean, of Regina, remembers her feelings: "That savage wind tormented me for nights on end . . . Oh, my God, I wanted so much to be back in my little house in Bancesti, in Bucovina. To see my sweet cherry trees which had been 100-foot tall in 1906 when I had gone away. Two sweet cherry trees, two lime trees and two walnut trees. I wonder if they are still there. Suffice it to know that Russia laid hands on them in 1944."

Returning to the Homeland

Although most Romanian immigrants adjusted to life in America, about one-third returned to their homeland, usually solitary men who had not come over in a group and formed no binding attachments. One of those disheartened by America was Nick Tecau, who left the new land, but not forever, as he explained in his interview:

> We wrecked big mountains of stone over there [in
> Ilasco, Missouri] . . . . My brother drilled a hole at
> night-time. . . . and it exploded and that's how he was
> killed. He was Avram Tecau, four years older than me.

Meantime I brought my older brother here, Simion. And after three years, we decided there was nothing but dark days here, you know, so we went home . . . . Then in 1912 I came back.

Other immigrants returned to Romania not because they failed in North America but because they enjoyed showing their old acquaintances how well their adventure had paid off. *An American in the Making* describes the return of one such man, Couza, whom Ravage also calls "the prophet from America." Ravage and other

Once established in American communities, many Romanian Americans became white-collar professionals, such as these import brokers in Philadelphia.

Romanian-American Nick Todea ran this café and liquor store in Cleveland in the early 1900s.

acquaintances of Couza remembered him as a "slouchy, unprepossessing youngster, with his toes out of his gaping boot-tips, carrying heavy cans of milk around for his mother." But after 14 years in the United States, Couza came back with jewels sparkling on his tie and on his fingers and with a gold neck chain studded with diamonds.

Despite this obvious display of wealth, Couza was a modest man in some respects. He refused to check into the big local hotel, staying instead with his brother and sharing the family's humble living space. Nor did Couza ever speak openly of his wealth; rather, he commented on it through his actions, such as contributing large sums of money to charities.

Couza's return utterly changed his small town. Those who had grown resigned to a bleak future in Romania looked forward to making a fresh start in America. As Ravage puts it: "A star had risen in heaven to lead us out of the wilderness." Before Couza's return, America had always been thought of as a place to run away to. One villager, Ravage writes, had run off to America and left his wife to beg in the streets. A man who had gone off to America was like a man dead—until Couza returned.

Romanians brought back news about life in Canada, too. An article in the June 20, 1890, issue of the *Prince Albert Times*, a newspaper in the little town of Prince Albert, Saskatchewan, describes the visit of Dr. Joseph Klemm, of Romania. Dr. Klemm, a teacher of agriculture, came to investigate the possibility of setting up Romanian colonies in Manitoba and the western territories. He had come across the sea to find out for himself whether Saskatchewan was really a "Siberia of America," as it was thought of at that time in eastern Europe.

Dr. Klemm was pleased with what he saw. He stated: "Instead of 'Siberia of America,' I find a well-developed country enjoying a healthy climate and a soil capable of producing an almost unlimited food supply . . . ." What exciting news this was for the Romanians, who had been awaiting assurances that would inspire them to make preparations for their trip to the new land. Dr. Klemm was so impressed with the virgin lands of western Canada that he wrote to some Romanians in the United States: "The territories are large enough and good enough for the whole of you."

Rapid Strides

In the first decade of the 20th century, unskilled laborers continued to constitute the majority in Romanian-

American communities. Before long, however, some immigrants had saved enough money to open small businesses—restaurants, bars, pool halls, even banks. By the early 1920s, the sons of these small businessmen had landed white-collar posts in large corporations.

Romanian Americans who continued to work at industrial jobs often joined trade unions but shied away from the socialist movement that, in the early 1900s, caught fire among many other immigrants, such as Italians, Jews, and Swedes. In 1913–14, however, a Romanian-American socialist group formed and enlisted with the Industrial Workers of the World (IWW), an organization that sought to unite all laborers for the purpose of overthrowing capitalism through peaceful

Many Romanian Americans joined the trade union movement, which culminated in a strike by Pennsylvania coal miners in 1900. Two years later President Theodore Roosevelt appointed the arbitration commission pictured here.

means, such as strikes, boycotts, and propaganda. Membership among Romanian Americans remained sparse: the average Romanian immigrant was more concerned with bettering himself through the system than agitating for its downfall.

Ethnic clubs sponsored activities including folk dances performed by Romanian Americans such as the Chicago troupe pictured in this 1934 photograph.

Community Spirit

Although few Romanian Americans felt drawn toward the fellowship of socialism, the group, as a whole, enjoyed the fraternal atmosphere of clubs, especially mutual benefit societies. These were institutions that helped immigrants acclimate themselves to life in the New World. The first such society, *Carpatina* (The Carpathian), was formed in 1902 in Cleveland. Its main purpose was to provide for Romanian-American immigrants in the event disaster struck. For a monthly fee, the immigrant received a guarantee that should he die, a fixed sum of money would go to his family.

Another Romanian-American club, *Societatea Romane de Ajutor si Cultura* (Romanian Society of Assistance and Culture), or RSAC, began in 1903 in Homestead, Pennsylvania. The RSAC came into existence as a result of frequent accidents that occurred on industrial sites. Many similar agencies sprang up soon after. As with the mutual benefit societies, members

Romania's Orthodox Catholics worshiped in elaborate churches such as this one, built by a 16th-century Walachian prince.

Devout Romanian Americans constructed rudimentary places of worship. This photo shows the Romanian Orthodox church of Gary, Indiana, in 1925.

paid a monthly fee in return for indemnity money that ranged at first between $100 and $200 and later climbed to $700. Before long, various societies banded together, linking the many Romanian-American communities scattered across the nation. By 1911, 44 organizations had joined a central group, the Union of Romanian Beneficial and Cultural Societies (USRA), headquartered in Newark, Ohio, where a USRA newspaper was published.

Not all the societies joined the USRA. In 1912 self-styled "intellectuals" in the Romanian-American work-

American Orthodox Romanians welcomed their first bishop, Policarp Morusca, in 1935.

ers' movement formed their own central organization, called *Liga De Ajutor,* or League of Assistance; this society openly competed with the USRA for members, and relations between the groups became acrimonious

and even violent. Finally, in 1928, the two mended their differences by forming the Union and League of Romanian Societies in America. Its initial membership totaled 6,500, less than 3 percent of the Romanian-American population, though a higher percentage than it claimed at any later time.

Despite the merging of the two clubs, the rift in the community between the "intellectuals" and other workers never really healed. In the 1930s and 1940s tensions persisted, often reflecting disputes that traced back to problems in Romania, which suffered continual political upheaval at this time. After World War II, tensions mounted again as a new wave of Romanian immigrants, more educated and more political than the earlier generation of newcomers, arrived on America's shores. Their story will be told in the next chapter.

The Church

Religious worship, central to Romanian life in Europe, gained new expression in America. Until 1905, however, Orthodox Romanians had no churches of their own and had to attend the somewhat different services held by Greeks, Serbs, or Russians. When such services did not exist, Romanian immigrants met in boarding-houses or even bars to worship. In 1905, the Orthodox parish of St. Mary's was founded in Cleveland. Soon after, a Romanian church leader, Reverend Moise Balea, came to America and founded 15 churches in other parts of the United States. Romanian immigrants finally had places of their own to worship in.

Just as the number of Romanian Orthodox churches increased, so, too, did friction—between parishes and between priests. Clerics ordained in the old country held views that conflicted with those of priests ordained in America. Similarly, Romanian Americans objected to the influence exerted by Hungarians over the Metro-politinate of Sibiu, the organization that had authority over the Romanian-American churches. In addition, because the Romanian protopope, or dean, of the American parishes sympathized with the Socialist party, many parishes in the New World refused to obey him and demanded that a separate Romanian-American episcopate be established. In 1929, their wish was granted, and their first bishop, Policarp Morusca, arrived in 1935.

The next year, Bishop Morusca founded a newspaper—*Solia* (the *Herald*) and an annual almanac, *Calendarul Solia* (the *Herald Calendar*), and in 1937 he arranged for the purchase of a 200-acre estate in Grass Lake, Michigan, which became the national headquarters for the episcopate. Two years later, Bishop Morusca traveled to Romania for a conference and was trapped there when World War II broke out. Hostilities concluded in 1945, but Morusca could not persuade the repressive Romanian government to let him return to the United States.

In 1950 the American churches divided. The majority, aligned with the Romanian Orthodox Episcopate of America (ROEA), broke off from those who followed Akron priest Andrei Moldovan, who had the backing of the new Romanian government. Once it became clear that Bishop Morusca would not be allowed to return from Romania, the ROEA leaders, or autonomists, elected Viorel B. Trifa as their bishop. He was consecrated as Bishop Valerian in Philadelphia in 1952 and charged with supervising the ROEA's 46 parishes and 10,000 members. He guarded the autonomy of the ROEA until 1960, when it merged with the Metropolia, the Russian Orthodox church in the United States. In 1970, the Metropolia became the Orthodox Church in America; the ROEA remained a partner in this self-governing affiliation. The Romanian bishop today belongs to the Holy Synod of the American Orthodox Church (formerly the Orthodox Church of America).

Meanwhile, the followers of Moldovan charted their own course. They named themselves the Romanian

Orthdox Missionary Episcopate of America (ROMEA) and named Victorian Ursache as their bishop, in 1966. In 1987 ROMEA had only 10 parishes in the United States, comprising about 500 family members and 1,500 single communicants.

Not all Romanian Americans remained strictly within the Romanian Orthododox church. In 1919, another sect arose—the Union of Greek Catholic Romanians in Northern America. In 1948, in Youngstown, Ohio, this group was reorganized as the Association of Romanian Catholics of America (ARCA) and claimed

In 1924 the editorial board of The American-Romanian Review *gathered for this portrait. At one time, 37 different Romanian-language publications rolled off American presses.*

about 1,500 members. Membership grew slowly; by the 1970s, about 4,300 Romanians belonged to the sect. Romanian Catholics have repeatedly asked the Vatican to appoint them a bishop, but have not yet been given one. Currently, the church sponsors cultural events, assists Romanian refugees, works with youths, and even serves as an insurance company.

Yet another sect, the first Romanian Baptist Church, was established in 1910 in Cincinnati. Three years later this church was reorganized as the Romanian Baptist Association. Since World War II the number of its parishes has fallen from 20 to 9, and by the 1970s the church claimed only about 2,500 adherents. Other Romanian Americans belong to one of several Romanian Protestant Pentecostals. In addition, there are five independent Orthodox churches. Throughout the 20th century, membership has declined among all Romanian religious groups, though in an effort to boost attendance, many churches have installed English for at least part of the liturgy, and youth activities have become a priority.

The Press

Today few Romanian-language daily newspapers are published in the United States, although Romanian Americans continue to support the foreign-language press. But in earlier times as many as 37 different Romanian-language newspapers, weeklies, and monthlies appeared in this country. Before 1930 two newspapers found special popularity: *Romanul*, for the educated immigrants, and *America*, an English-language periodical for the working classes. After 1930 *America* was the favorite of both groups—it was still published as of 1987, as a biweekly.

Among journals the most popular during World War II was the *New Pioneer*, which strongly supported Romanian culture and American ideals. In the 1950s a number of anticommunist journals appeared as well as

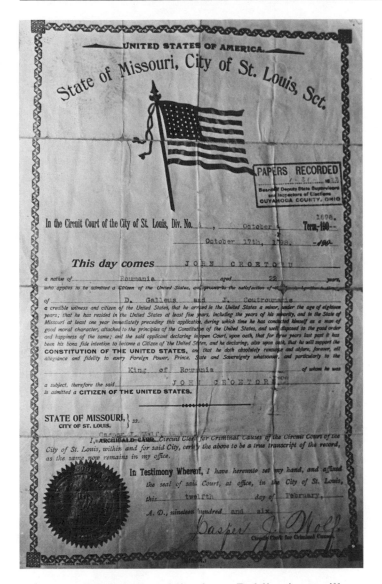

Many Romanian immigrants who planned to return to their homeland with their earnings instead became United States citizens.

a few pro-Bucharest publications. Publications still active in the 1980s included the monthly *Romanian Bulletin*, distributed by the Romanian Library in New York, and the *American-Romanian Review*, published in Cleveland by the American Romanian Heritage Foundation. ⬿

In the 1980s many Romanian immigrants congregated in Sunnyside, a neighborhood in the New York City borough of Queens.

THE NOI-VENITI

Since World War II Romanian politics have been deeply affected by the adversarial relationship between the United States and the Soviet Union. One consequence of this relationship has been that the Romanian government has obeyed the Soviet Union by cracking down on emigration. Economic considerations, however, have forced Romania to court the favor of the United States, in the hope of obtaining Most Favored Nation status, which would relax trade restrictions and open commerce between the countries. In 1975, Romania achieved this goal after agreeing to loosen its emigration policies. However, "free emigration" still has an ambiguous meaning, and official repression continues, albeit in milder form. Even so, a new generation of Romanian immigrants has moved to America.

Although the Romanian government has honored emigration requests for religious reasons, many people wish to go to America in order to rejoin their families. Having close relatives in another country increases their chances of being allowed to emigrate. Not all immigrants receive passports immediately: Sometimes the wait can drag on for five years, and spouses often endure year-long separations because one has been granted a passport in advance of the other. Immigrants often take up temporary residence in another country before obtaining a visa allowing them entry into the United States. Spain, France, and Austria harbor many Romanians whose ultimate goal is North America.

Though well educated in their homeland, noi-veniti *often face limited job prospects in the United States.*

A term coined by early Romanian immigrants describes those who came to America after World War II: *noi-veniti,* or "newly arrived." From the outset discomfort and distrust damaged the relationship between these two groups, in part because different circumstances caused the two groups to immigrate; also, different circumstances awaited them in America.

In the past, Romanians immigrants relied on institutions and organizations that eased their transition into American society. In the postwar era, however, fewer such agencies have been formed to assist the newly arrived. The Iuliu Maniu Foundation in New York aids immigrants, as do the Orthodox Brotherhood, Romanian Welfare, Inc., and the Cultural Association for Romanians and Americans of Romanian Descent. For Stefan Ralescu, a mathematician living in Riverdale, New York, the International Rescue Committee (IRC) proved of great value. IRC officials met him at Kennedy airport, shepherded him to a New York City hotel, and made all the arrangements for his transportation to Bloomington, Indiana, where a teaching position awaited him.

Whereas many cities once had them, Romanian neighborhoods have disappeared, by and large. Instead of merging into an active immigrant community, the newly arrived stay with a few friends or relatives and live with them until an apartment is found, preferably nearby. The immigrants find out immediately, to their relief, that the standard of living in America is higher than in Romania.

An In-depth Interview

On a muggy evening in June 1987, George and Tatiana Stratomir sat on folding chairs in an unfurnished apartment in Queens, New York, and patiently answered questions about their experience in America. They arrived in 1983, and during the next four years George pumped gas, drove a taxi, and finally got work as a laboratory technician. This last job enabled the couple to move into a larger apartment but gave George little contentment. In Romania, he had been a surgeon, specializing in anesthesiology and nephrology (the medical study of the kidneys).

Recalling her apartment in Romania, Tatiana Stratomir told an interviewer:

> It took us two years to pay for all that furniture. Even though George was a doctor, the place wasn't very stylish. It was very cheap, modest. When we came here, we didn't have money, but it was easier to furnish our apartment than as a doctor over there. Everything is easier to buy.

Her husband seconded this view, adding, "I think here there are no poor people, really—compared to Romania."

Émigré photographer Alfred Kaufmann, a resident of Queens, photographed this local bakery in 1987.

Unlike the first Romanian immigrants, who spoke no English when they arrived, many noi-veniti have studied English at school in Romania. Their familiarity with the language helps explain their independence from Romanian-American organizations. The newly arrived are seldom easy prey for those looking to fleece greenhorns and, as a result, have little need for others to protect them. Yet even those who do not speak English keep their distance from the organizations. They seem to prefer surviving on their own, although the route can be lonely. As George Stratomir put it, "When I came here, I didn't like it. I couldn't communicate, didn't understand. I learned from the tape recorder and books, in my room, alone. After six months, I started to communicate and I started to like it a little."

In an article published in the May–June 1978 issue of *American-Romanian Review*, Valentin Hurgoia offered an interesting explanation for the reluctance of the noi-veniti to become involved with immigrant agencies. Hurgoia blames the totalitarian regime currently governing Romania, which rules by dictate and force, compelling citizens to belong to one organization or another. Once they come to America, which demands no such participation, immigrants gratefully exercise their freedom of choice at the cost of remaining isolated.

Finding Work

Noi-veniti tend to be well-educated urban professionals. In Romania many were teachers, journalists, lawyers, doctors, and engineers. But work experience in Romania does not always carry much weight in America. For the newly arrived who have specialized vocations, the options can be distressingly narrow. Most newcomers, in fact, face a situation akin to Tatania Stratomir's. After working in Romania as an architect, she managed to become a draftsperson in the United States, but only after months of study. "The main prob-

The noi-veniti *worship according to ancient custom at St. Mary's, a Romanian Orthodox church in Queens.*

lem," she explained, "is the English language, spoken and professional." Alfred Kaufmann, a photographer in New York, ranked among Romania's top photographers, receiving assignments from magazines equivalent to *Time* or *Newsweek*. In America, however, he has struggled to find work worthy of his talent.

A different fate greeted Stefan Ralescu, the mathematician from Riverdale. While waiting to emigrate from Paris—where he lodged temporarily—Ralescu arranged for a position at a university in the United States. This planning made his lot considerably easier than it might otherwise have been.

Few Romanian Americans have gotten off to as promising a beginning in North America as Dan Costin. Born on June 11, 1965, Dan was given an American-sounding name by his parents, who had enjoyed the exploits of a cowboy in a Hollywood film that ran in their town, Iasi, in northeastern Romania. Because they were Jewish, the Costins faced persecution and job dis-

Traditional Romanian-American weddings include the "Kissing Dance," in which the guests twist their napkins into blindfolds.

crimination in Romania, and it seemed the same fate might await Dan. So in 1977 the family immigrated to the United States, taking up residence in New York City. Costin enrolled in the Bronx High School of Science, a prestigious public school, and was introduced there to computers. "I would probably not have been involved in computer science in Romania," he said in 1987, "because the field is in such early stages of development and high school students don't get a chance to work with computers."

After high school, Costin entered Harvard University and devised his own course of study called computational neuroscience which enabled him to use computers to examine the brain. During his investigations he created a software program that could be used to measure visual responses; this program proved so successful that Costin formed a company that sold the software to psychology laboratories.

In 1987, Dan graduated from Harvard and found a job developing artificial intelligence software for International Business Machines (IBM) in Menlo Park, California. Today when he visits his family in Scarsdale, New York, Dan speaks Romanian and hears about current Romanian culture from his father, who maintains

contacts with his homeland through his own business—
trading perfume with Eastern bloc nations. Although
glad to be an American, Dan retains strong ties to Romania. "I can't forget the country I lived in for half my
life," he explained. "Being raised in two countries
makes me realize there are two ways of living and both
ways are fine."

Reaching Out

Just as the noi-veniti refrain from joining fraternal societies, so they often also have no strong religious affiliation. One reason may be that Soviet-controlled
Eastern bloc countries disapprove of all churches. Another reason harks back to a situation common among
the first wave of Romanian immigrants: Few appropri-
ate congregations exist for them in America. The newer
immigrants have little problem finding an actual place
to worship, but they have less success locating similar
people to worship with. Tatiana Stratomir put this
quandary in a revealing light:

> Romania now allows low people to come here, like the
> people who left Cuba, people who are uneducated
> . . . They come to our church and we avoid them . . .
> Last time, Easter, was a bad experience. People
> screamed, were noisy on the street, as if the event was
> a party. So we don't go to church anymore because
> we avoid them.

George added that the couple now preferred Greek Orthodox or Catholic churches.
    Friends constitute their most vital resource. After
arriving in America, immigrants seek out old acquaintances from Romania. They speak the same language,
share similar experiences in the new land, and help each
other with difficulties. They learn English together and
together take their first tentative steps into American
society. Though George Stratomir learned English on
his own and very slowly, he found that most of his

fellow immigrants were sympathetic, as were other Americans: "This is the marvelous thing of America," he commented. "In Spain I traveled, in Italy, and everywhere I felt like an outsider. But in America, no."

But just as early immigrants noticed that America had changed those who preceded them to the New World, so also do the noi-veniti feel like outsiders in the company of more established Romanian Americans. As Tatiana put it:

> You won't find the same person here that you found over there. But it's normal to change. You come from old mentality to new mentality. What is this new mentality? The word used most often is "money." "How much does it cost?" Oh, it costs too much! They don't dream anymore. They are not so sophisticated. I never hear them talk about books.

The gulf between the old mentality and the new is often bridged by humor. As Kenneth Thigpen explains in *Folklore and the Ethnicity Factor in the Lives of Romanian Americans*, political jokes serve to unite recent and older immigrants together in their almost universal contempt for the difficulties of life in the old country and to make them feel closer to one another in the new land. A joke may jab at the paradox of a certain aspect of life under the Communists, or, as in the following example, it may make a direct hit on communist leaders: President Nicolae Ceausescu meets with his principal assistant, Ion Gheorghe Maurer. The topic of discussion is the opening of Romania's borders for emigration. Ceausescu worries that if the borders are opened, no one in the country will be left but the two of them. Maurer pauses, then responds, "If the borders were open, President Ceausescu, then *you* would be the only one left."

Hardships

Despite being, on the whole, better educated and more sophisticated than the first immigrant wave, the noi-

Many recent Romanian immigrants keep abreast of events in their homeland by reading foreign-language publications.

veniti endure many of the same difficulties faced by their forebears. For example, they often feel estranged from their families back in Romania, who must adapt to life without the immigrant as the immigrant must adapt to America. This difference in their experiences often drives a wedge between them; as Tatiana explained: "Most of the families are separated, after they come and meet again together, they meet like two strangers . . . . They relate in different ways . . . . In time, if they work hard, they get along. If you are not so strong, it's the end."

At the same time, the newly arrived, like the older immigrants, miss those family members who will never join them. George and Tatiana regret that they will probably never again see their mothers, who are of advanced age and frail health and would have difficulty obtaining passports. The Stratomirs also have resigned themselves to losing touch with close Romanian friends, possibly forever. Tatiana put the matter philosophically: "I don't write them anymore. But they are with me, they don't betray me. They follow me—it's all been established. And I'm sure if I see them after 20 years, it'll be the same."

Like earlier immigrants, noi-veniti sometimes feel at odds with their new neighbors, especially those who seem ignorant not only of Romanian culture but even of the country's location on the map. Tatiana recalled speaking with a co-worker who confused Romania with Bulgaria, and Stefan Ralescu admitted that sometimes he wished he could educate Americans who know noth-

George Zolnay supervised the sculptures at the St. Louis World's Fair, shown here from above in 1904.

ing about Romania. To immigrants, this ignorance reflects the overall failure of the American educational system, which is less rigorous than Romania's, especially at the grade-school level.

"My daughter in sixth grade and doesn't know Shaw or Dickens," Tatania told the interviewer. "Not even American writers . . . They don't develop logical thinking . . . I want to give her a better education. Sending her to friends in Spain, for one month to learn second language." When asked if the American elementary schools had anything valuable to offer, Tatiana thought for a moment. "Maybe here," she said, "they teach more about human ways, instead of lots of information."

A Romanian Canadian

In 1974, two years after leaving Romania for France, Mariuca Ralescu and her family sought to proceed to North America. American immigration officials in Paris, however, seemed suspicious of her parents for having joined the Communist Party in Romania—a move, Mariuca explained, made by many citizens wanting to better their standard of living. Fortunately, Canadian officials showed more sympathy. They were "much nicer, softer," Mariuca recalled. "They didn't care that much about the Communist party, they were just interested to know if my parents could find work." That experience set the tone for her stay in Canada: "I felt it was my home. I felt good in Montreal."

Like newcomers to the United States, Mariuca's parents struggled to fit into the workplace, and Mariuca longed for the companionship of a tight-knit community. In Canada, "Romanians don't have Romanian schools, they don't congregate, they're not like the Spanish. Even the Hungarians and Russians all have communities." Eight months after arriving in Montreal, however, Mariuca discovered a sense of community that she had not anticipated. Her reminiscence must be a familiar one to noi-veniti in Canada and America alike:

> I came to New York in 1976. We went to Central Park. There was a concert. I was able to compare the attitudes of the people going to concerts in Romania with these people in America. In the Communist country you're so introverted. You can't let go of your feeling. In Central Park it was a riot. I started to cry. I would've liked to express myself the same way but I wasn't free yet . . . You see the abundance of food and clothes right away, but after a while you see it's not the most important thing—it's the way people feel and act.

Here To Stay

At the conclusion of his interview, George Stratomir suddenly looked at his watch, then rushed out of his chair and into the next room. It was 11:00 P.M. and he was half an hour late for his shift at the lab. As he bustled about the apartment, gathering his things, his wife tried to sum up their experiences thus far in America: "I still feel like European, but I'm trying to get to the American mentality and the way they can decide their life, which is beautiful." George reentered the room and hurriedly shook hands with the interviewer, who posed one last question: Did the Stratomirs ever feel like returning to Romania, like some of the Romanian immigrants early in the century? Tatania quickly spoke up. "I can return anytime," she said. "But George can't." She reminded the interviewer that because George defected, he can never again return to Romania. (Tatania can return because she left the country to rejoin her husband, not to register a political protest.) George, on his way out, paused. "In my mind I can't give up, to accept another job. One time, I'll be a doctor again."

The door shut and he left. Tatiana explained that George must first pass one more exam, then complete the three required years of residency. She fell quiet,

then tried to summarize the reasons why she and her husband—and many of the noi-veniti—decided to leave Romania for the new land: "What's the truth—we haven't found it yet. We were on a platform, couldn't get higher. To have more life. Maybe we left to be more alive."

Bela and Marta Karolyi (center) meet with Texas congressman Bill Archer (right), who arranged for the couple's young daughter to leave Romania.

A Century of Achievers

Perhaps nothing binds the disparate segments of the Romanian-American population more closely than its collective pride in the achievements of certain members of the community. Romanian Americans can look back on a long record of accomplishment—one that predates the first immigrant wave of the late 19th century. During the Civil War, Gheorge Pomutz, a member of the

Bela Karolyi congratulates Mary Lou Retton, whom he coached to a gold medal in the 1984 Olympics.

Iowa Volunteer Regiment, rose to the rank of brigadier general. After the war ended, President Andrew Johnson appointed Pomutz to the post of U.S counsel general to Russia.

Another war hero was Nicolae Dunca. Born in Iasi, Romania, in 1837, Dunca joined the military as a career officer, then came to the United States shortly after the Civil War began. In 1862 Dunca was made captain of the U.S. Volunteers from New York State. Assigned to Wheeling, West Virginia, he served as aide-de-camp to the Union army's General John Frémont. On June 8, 1862, General Stonewall Jackson and his Confederate forces defeated Frémont's army at Cross Keys. One hundred and twenty-five men died, including Captain

Dunca. "Of my staff I lost a good and courageous officer—killed—Captain Nicolae Dunca," wrote General Frémont in his report to the secretary of war. Another Romanian-American volunteer reported the circumstances of Dunca's death, recalling that late in the afternoon on the day of the battle, Dunca was ordered to go to the front to survey and inspect the situation. He was not seen alive again. Later, his body was found, riddled with bullets. His funeral was held the next day with full military honors.

In 1863—not long after Dunca was killed in battle—another Romanian American, George Zolnay, was born in Romania. After graduating with honors from the Royal Art Institute in Bucharest, he immigrated to New York, then went to St. Louis, where he served as head of the sculpture division of the art department at the 1903 World's Fair. Later Zolnay became the director of the University City Arts Academy, also in St. Louis, and later still he moved to Washington, D.C. His principal works include the Confederate monument in Forest Park, St. Louis; the figures on the U.S. Court House, San Francisco; and busts of Emperor Francis Joseph, French author Victor Hugo, and General "Stonewall" Jackson. Eventually Zolnay was decorated by the king of Romania. He died in May 1949 and was buried in New York.

Author Peter Neagoe was born in 1881, in Odorheiu, Transylvania. At the age of 17 he went to Bucharest to study painting and befriended the great Romanian sculptor Constantin Brancusi. In 1905 Neagoe boarded a ship bound for North America, arriving with only a silver dollar in his pocket. He worked at various jobs to support his painting and diligently improved his knowledge of the English language. In 1911 he married a Lithuanian immigrant who was also a painter, and the couple went to Paris, where they joined the community of American writers that included Ernest Hemingway, Henry Miller, and Gertrude Stein. In

1932 Neagoe published his first collection of short stories, *Storm*. Two years later he assembled an anthology, *American Abroad*. Neagoe continued to divide his time between the United States and Europe until his death in 1960. He wrote a number of books containing nostalgic evocations of Transylvania. His publications include *Winning a Wife* (1935); *There Is My Heart* (1936); *A Time to Keep* (1949); and *No Time for Tears* (1958).

Champion Coaches

The roster of Romanian Americans also includes some who rose to prominence in the old country. Two such are Bela and Marta Karolyi. They met in the early 1960s, when both were student-athletes in Cluj, Romania. After marrying in 1963, they opened a school for aspiring gymnasts. Their students included a young girl named Nadia Comeneci, who showed remarkable talent. The Karolyis worked daily with her, molding her into the champion whose lithe artistry delighted the world during the 1976 Olympics, in which she won three gold medals. Thereafter, Comeneci's standing eroded somewhat, and the Romanian team suffered, finishing behind the Soviet Union at the 1980 Olympics. The Romanian Gymnastics Federation, disappointed with the Karolyis, blamed them for developing a troubled relationship with the star they had discovered and shaped. As punishment, the Karolyis' program lost some of its funding.

Events came to a head on March 30, 1981, during the Karolyis' exhibition tour of the United States. At 3:00 A.M., in a New York City hotel room, the couple decided to defect. Difficulties arose, however. They first had to spend a week with American immigration officials, answering a battery of questions. They then had to wait a week before they could speak with their 8-year-old daughter, Andrea, who was back in Romania. Distraught by this separation, the Karolyis enlisted the aid of Texan Bill Archer, a member of the

U.S. House of Representatives. Congressman Archer arranged for Andrea's departure from Romania, and soon she was reunited with her parents.

Because of their reputation as teachers, the Karolyis quickly found jobs at the University of Oklahoma, in Norman. They also taught at a local club there and ran summer clinics. Bela Karolyi's success training young American gymnasts has equaled, perhaps even surpassed, his triumphs in Romania. The best known of his protégés, Mary Lou Retton, captured the hearts of many with her gold-medal performance in the 1984 Olympics. Her accomplishment inspired legions of young girls to take up the sport, many of them dreaming of the day when they too will come under the tutelage of the great Romanian-American coach. Indeed, Karolyi himself has become a celebrity whose face appears often in print and on television.

In 1974 Dr. George Palade won the Nobel Prize for his discovery of ribosomes.

John Houseman's many theatrical successes include the Acting Company, a touring troupe he founded in 1972.

Contemporary Thinkers and Artists

Mircea Eliade, one of the leading intellectuals of the mid-20th century, was born in Bucharest on March 9, 1907, and studied in Italy and India, where he became an apprentice yogi. When World War II erupted, he served as Romania's cultural attaché in London. After the war ended, he taught in Paris. He came to this country at age 50 and assumed a teaching post at the University of Chicago Divinity School. There he wrote many highly acclaimed studies about religion and mythology and eventually was named the Sewell L. Avery Distinguished Service Professor. He also belonged to the university's Committee on Social Thought, whose members included such luminaries as Nobel Prize–winning novelist Saul Bellow. Eliade died in 1986.

In *Mircea Eliade: Ordeal By Labyrinth*, interviewer Claude Henri Rocquet persuaded his subject to comment at length about America and Americans. At one point Eliade offered this observation:

> Chicago stands in the middle of a plain that stretches for hundreds and hundreds of miles; every now and then there is a city and wealthy residential neighborhoods, rather like artificial Gardens of Eden—beautiful houses, but people just shut themselves away in them, and it's all rather artificial.
> . . . What I like about America, to take one example, is the importance given to the wife . . . the first thing they asked me was whether my wife liked it there. The attention paid to the wife, the family, that's something I like very much . . . .
> Americans are quite justifiably accused of a great many things, but there are a lot of admirable things about them that are seldom mentioned; for example, their extremely tolerant attitude in religious and spiritual matters.

Another intellectual, Dr. George Palade, was born in Iasi, Romania, in 1912, and immigrated to the United States in 1946. A founder and editor of the *Journal of Cell Biology*, Dr. Palade won the Nobel Prize in 1974 (along with two other scientists) for his discovery of ribosomes, the protein synthesizers of molecular cells.

John Houseman, the producer, actor, and director, was born Jacques Haussman in Bucharest, in 1902. He studied at Clifton College in England, then came to the United States, where he ran the Mercury Theater in the 1930s, collaborating with Orson Welles (best known for directing and starring in the 1941 film classic *Citizen Kane*). Together, Houseman and Welles introduced new vitality to the American theater, and Houseman won plaudits for his versions of *Hamlet* and for the stage version of *Native Son*, Richard Wright's scathing account of the Afro-American experience.

In the 1950s, Houseman served as artistic director of the American Shakespeare Festival, and from the late 1960s through the mid-1970s he headed the drama division of the Juilliard School in New York City. Most Americans know Houseman for his Oscar-winning portrayal of an intimidating Harvard Law School professor in the 1974 film and subsequent television series *The Paper Chase*. In 1975 he founded the Acting Company, a national repertory theater group that tours the United States, giving performances of classic and contemporary stage works. Houseman has recorded his stage experiences in several highly acclaimed books, including *Final Dress* and *Run-Through*.

Another Romanian American whose innovations have changed the theater is Andrei Serban. Born in Bucharest in 1943, the son of a photographer and a schoolteacher, Serban gained admittance into the prestigious Institute of Theatrical and Cinematographic Arts in Bucharest. After training there, he became Romania's most controversial interpreter of classical theater. In 1965 Serban headed to America at the urging of an American visitor and with the help of a Ford Foundation grant.

At first Serban had trouble with the English language and could communicate only in French and with hand gestures. In time, however, he made his mark on the avant-garde theater in New York. His directorial debut, *Arden of Feversham* (possibly authored by Shakespeare), earned triumphant reviews when it was staged at the La Mama Experimental Theatre Club in New York City in 1970. A year later his production of the ancient Greek classic *Medea* won the highly esteemed

Andrei Serban, a controversial director in Romania, made his mark on American avant-garde theater soon after he defected in 1965.

Drama Desk Award. Serban went on to stage imaginative versions of Shakespeare's *Romeo and Juliet* and *Electra*, another ancient Greek masterpiece. He has often toured internationally and in the United States has been aided with grants from the Rockefeller and Guggenheim foundations. ❧

Romanian Americans in Youngstown, Ohio, display their dual heritage in a 1953 celebration.

FORGETTING AND REMEMBERING

I rina Kaufmann, who left Romania at age 8 and arrived in this country in 1962, once recalled her introduction to a peculiar form of New York City restaurant—the "automat." "We never had that in Romania," she said. "All these little sandwiches popping out of these little boxes with windows in them. It was amazing." For Irina the automat provided more than a novel eating experience: It symbolized the diversity of choices available to American immigrants. In the villages and towns where most Romanian immigrants grew up, the future held few options. This limitation ultimately sent many people to the New World in search of greater opportunity. Once they arrived they found that the diversity of experience made it more difficult to forge bonds with other Romanian Americans. The multiplicity of choices, in other words, turned them into strangers, often forgetful of their ties to the Old World.

Today's Romanian Americans alternate forgetfulness with remembrance. Forgetfulness sometimes leads them to overlook their ancestral origins as they plunge into mainstream American society. For many members of the community, the Romanian language, church, and customs no longer seem crucial to their identity. Others willingly acknowledge the past—the European as well as the immigrant past—and value its relevance to their present and future experiences.

Forgetting

Every ethnic group in North America faces the dilemma of assimilation, the process that causes unique people to lose their distinctive cultural traits as they come to resemble their neighbors. The *Harvard Encyclopedia of American Ethnic Groups* lists several metaphors—or analogies—describing this aspect of American life: melting pot, salad bowl, mosaic, crucible, symphonic orchestration. These metaphors raise questions about what it means to be an American. Are we people who feel burdened by the cultural heritage we bring from foreign lands? Are we forever striving to renounce the past and become "new beings," tailoring ourselves to fit a common pattern? These questions, posed at one time or another by many Americans, can be traced back to the beginnings of the nation. For example, the American jurist and statesman John Jay, in *The Federalist* papers of 1787, called for all Americans to adopt the language and customs of the English.

By and large, Romanian Americans agree with this view. Indeed, Romanian Americans have assimilated quickly. Josef Barton's *Peasants and Strangers* cites a member of Cleveland's Romanian-American community who in 1906 drew attention to the problem: "There are no Romanian schools, nor can there be, because the families don't support them. One generation, at most two, and there will be no more Romanians."

At the same time that Romanian Americans seek to become "100 percent American," many desire to keep their old culture alive. This ambivalence is expressed by Stefan Ralescu, who immigrated to America at age 25, then had to decide how to raise his two young daughters:

> I would like to teach my children about Romanian culture. I think it's good for children to know their parents' background. We speak Romanian, we cook Romanian, we have memories and friends. I would tell

[my daughter Melanie] about Scufita Rosie (Little
Red Riding Hood)—stories, folktales we grew up with.
I don't want her to keep the same tradition [I grew up
in]. But our culture is Romanian, we'd like our children
to understand where we're coming from.

Intermarriage also poses a problem. Barton's *Peasants and Strangers* notes that each generation of Romanian Americans is more likely than the preceding one to marry outside the ethnic group. Often a Romanian American will wed someone from another ethnic community that has been in the country about the same length of time. Thus husband and wife face similar conflicts and feel equally torn between the Old World—embodied in their parents' values—and the new. Another bond is often supplied by religion: Romanians have tended to marry people who share their own faith—if not some form of Orthodox Christianity, then Roman Catholic. This practice continues today.

In Canada assimilation has proceeded more slowly because the first Romanian immigrants there settled, for the most part, in the rural areas of the country's western provinces. But as time passed, the prospect of greater economic opportunity drew them to the cities, where they have faced conditions similar to those met by their compatriots in the United States; the great variety of urban experience, its sophistication, and its crowded housing throw together people of diverse backgrounds, creating a universe of intimate strangers.

Even outside the cities, Romanian Canadians have seen their distinct ethnicity wane. G. James Patterson's *The Romanians of Saskatchewan: Four Generations of Adaptation*, explains that whereas the first and second generations of Romanians in this moderately populated province retained their Romanian identity, the third and fourth generations began to lose their ethnic "characteristics." Assimilation has not wholly erased the ancestral memories of Romanian Canadians, however. Patterson found that in the town of Regina, young peo-

Bishop Valerian—Viorel Trifa—collaborated with the Nazis during World War II, a sobering reminder of one aspect of the Romanian-American heritage.

ple showed interest in Romanian dances and in the annual Romanian spring festival. Patterson also noted that their knowledge of their culture comes not just from the lore passed down by their elders but also from the medium of books, records, and cultural events.

Remembering the past also means acknowledging distressing facts. Consider the case of Viorel Trifa. In

1950, he was admitted to the United States, and in 1952 he was consecrated as Bishop Valerian, so designated by the leaders of the Romanian Orthodox Episcopate of America, which included 46 parishes and 10,000 members. In 1982, under pressure from the federal government, Trifa admitted that he had concealed facts from immigration officials about his past. For example, in 1941 Trifa delivered an anti-Semitic speech that touched off 4 days of rioting in Bucharest during which 300 Jews and Christians were killed. He also admitted to editing an anti-Jewish newspaper and giving pro-Nazi speeches. Despite protests by some Romanian community leaders, Trifa was deported in 1982. He died in Portugal in 1987.

The Trifa case has created discomfort for Romanian Americans. Many would like to close their eyes and forget the incident. But few could ignore Trifa's comment, quoted in 1984 in the *New York Times*: "I am a man who happened to get put in a moment of history when some people wanted to make a point. The point was to revive the [memory of the] Holocaust. But all this talk by the Jews about the Holocaust is going to backfire." This hostile remark unwittingly summarizes the danger of forgetting. To ignore the past may pave the way for future persecution.

Remembering

Sunday, May 28, 1978, marked the inauguration of the Heritage Center at Grass Lake, Michigan. The event attracted hundreds of people, who shared in Romanian religious and social activities. Situated near the headquarters of the Romanian Orthodox Episcopate of America, the center includes a library, exhibition rooms, offices, and an apartment for a live-in director-researcher. The center was sponsored by the Romanian Orthodox Episcopate, but it operates independently and welcomes anyone interested in furthering the study, research, and documentation of Romanian

Americans and Romanian Canadians. The center, in sum, stands as a testament to the memory of Romanians in North America.

The act of remembering, however, does not take place only in institutions such as the Heritage Center, with its documents, card catalogs, and display cases. In their daily lives, Romanian Americans carry on the traditions of their homeland. Some weddings, for instance, still incorporate Romanian elements. One such ceremony has been described by the writer I. L. Popescu, who in the 1980s journeyed across Canada, intent on meeting Romanian Canadians and recording their stories. Popescu's account of "an old-fashioned Romanian wedding" focuses on the reception. It began after the party arrived at the Community Hall. The priest intoned the Lord's Prayer and blessed the food; then an unusual sound filled the room:

Romanian Orthodox clergy in Jackson, Michigan, participate in the church's annual July 4 assembly.

Four hundred people clicked their spoons against their plates to create the necessary background for the newlyweds' kiss. The newlyweds did kiss each other.

The number of decibels was bigger than near an international airport . . . They were barely seated when the inferno of spoons and forks mercilessly started again. Another kiss . . . [and] a one-hour supper followed.

Popescu reports that a few of the older guests were dismayed that some of the wedding customs had been abandoned, though many others had been kept. There was much dancing, old tunes were sung, the cinste was counted and applauded. Afterward, as the party broke up, the newlyweds held hands and bade good-bye to the guests. In the old country, Popescu notes, custom decreed that bride and groom be tied to one another with a *chischideu*, a hand towel embroidered with flowers. Popescu, like some of the older guests, laments the passing of old Romanian folkways—and comments in dramatic terms: "Farewell to the Romanian language! Farewell to the customs and ceremonials from the far-away Old Country of the grandparents!" These words echo those spoken in 1905, when the early immigrant couple, John and Maria Porea, had their wedding in Youngstown, Ohio. On that occasion, an older man, Mr. Dopu, stood up and recited a Romanian proverb that seemed to sum up the feelings of the assembled guests: "Don't leave an old good friend of yours in order to please a new one."

Perhaps Georgina and Tony—the newlyweds in Canada—have found the new land to be the friend that John and Maria, 80 years before, joyfully recognized; perhaps, for these later newlyweds, the old Romanian proverb has been turned around a little: Instead of trying to please their new friend, they've found that their new friend, North America, pleases them. Certainly, it has pleased many others. Romanian Americans have known hardship—struggling first to survive and then to avoid the loss of their unique identity. Most would agree, however, that the New World has been good to them. ✺

FURTHER READING

Barton, Josef. *Peasants and Strangers: Italians, Rumanians, and Slovaks in an American City, 1890–1950*. Cambridge: Harvard University Press, 1975.

Hurgoi, Valentin. *American Romanian Review*. Cleveland: American Romanian Heritage Foundation, May/June 1978.

Patterson, G. James. *The Romanians of Saskatchewan: Four Generations of Adaptation*. Ottawa: National Museum of Canada, 1977.

Popescu, I.L. *Land of Promise: Romanian Stories of Canadian Prairies*. Bucharest: The Romanian Association, 1986.

Porea, Cornelia. *The New Pioneer*, vol. 1, no. 2. Cleveland: The Cultural Association for Americans of Romanian Descent, February 1943.

Ravage, M. E. *An American in the Making*. New York: Dover, 1971.

Rocquet, Claude-Henri. *Mircea Eliade; Ordeal by Labyrinth*. Chicago: The University of Chicago Press, 1982.

Thigpen, Kenneth A. *Folklore and the Ethnicity Factor in the Lives of Romanian Americans*. New York: Arno Press, 1980.

Wertsman, Vladimir. *The Romanians in America, 1748–1974: A Chronology and Factbook*. New York: Oceana Publications, 1975.

——. *The Romanians in America and Canada: A Guide to Information Sources*. Detroit: Gale Research Co., 1980.

INDEX

Johnson, Andrew, 90
Journal of Cell Biology, 95

Karolyi, Andrea, 92–93
Karolyi, Bela, 92–93
Karolyi, Marta, 92–93
Kaufmann, Alfred, 81
Kaufmann, Irina, 96
Khrushchev, Nikita, 29
Klemm, Joseph, 65

Land of Promise (Popescu), 60–62
League of Assistance. *See* Liga de
  Ajutor
Liga de Ajutor, 70
Lipan, Tilly, 36–37
Lupastean, Dominica, 36, 62

Macedonia, 31–32
Magyars, 19
Maniu, Iuliu, 27
Marcus Aurelius, 17
Maurer, Ion Gheorghe, 84
Metropolitinate of Sibiu, 71
Michael, king of Romania, 29
Miller, Henry, 91
Mircea Eliade: Ordeal by Labyrinth
  (Rocquet), 95
Moldavia, 20–23, 31
Moldovan, Andrei, 72
Mongols, 19
Morusca, Policarp, 72
Muntean, Leona, 38

National Christian Party, 28
National Peasant Party, 27
Neagoe, Peter, 91–92
New Pioneer, 13
Noi-veniti, 78–81, 83–85, 88
No Time for Tears (Neagoe), 92

Orthodox Brotherhood, 78
Ottoman Empire. *See* Turkey

Palade, George, 95
Paris, Treaty of, 23

Patterson, G. James, 101–2
Peasants and Strangers (Barton),
  101–2
Phanariots, 21–22
Pomutz, Gheorge, 89
Popescu, I. L., 36, 60, 104–5
Porea, Cornelia, 13
Porea, John, 13–14, 105
Porea, Maria, 13–14, 105
Prince Albert Times, 65

Ralescu, Mariuca, 87, 100
Ralescu, Stefan, 81, 86
Ravage, M. E., 31, 35, 43, 63
Regina, Canada, 36–37
Retton, Mary Lou, 93
Rocquet, Claude Henri, 95
ROEA. *See* Romanian Orthodox
  Episcopate of America
Romanian Americans
  assimilation, 100–105
  avoided farming work, 47
  ethnic makeup, 32–33
  immigration after World War II,
    77–87
  legislation against immigrants,
    40–41
  passage to the New World, 36–38
  press, 74–75
  reasons for immigrating, 14–15,
    32–33
  religious worship, 71–74
Romanian Baptist Association, 74
Romanian Baptist church, 74
Romanian Bulletin, 25
Romanian Canadians, 60–62, 88–89
Romanian language, 18
Romanian Orthodox Episcopate of
  America, 72, 103
Romanian Orthodox Missionary
  Episcopate of America, 73
Romanian Orthodoxy in Youngstown
  (Bobango), 57
Romanian Society of Assistance and
  Culture. *See* Societatea Romane
  de Ajutor si Cultura

Picture credits

We would like to thank the following sources for providing photographs: AP/
Wide World Photos: pp. 25, 97; Art Resource: p. 16; Balch Institute for Ethnic
Studies: p. 63; The Bettmann Archive: pp. 21, 26; Carnegie Library of Pittsburgh:
p. 59; Eastfoto: p. 19; Editura Stiintiifica si Enciclopedica: pp. 20, 24, 68; Holy
Trinity Romanian Orthodox Church, Youngstown, Ohio: pp. 61, 70; Institute of
Texan Cultures: p. 34; Alfred Kaufmann: pp. 28, 49–56, 76, 78, 79, 81, 85;
Library of Congress: pp. 23, 35, 37, 38, 40, 42, 47, 48, 68; Louis Martin, Cleve-
land, Ohio: pp. 67, 69; Print Department, Boston Public Library: p. 32; Public
Archives of Canada: pp. 14, 46, 60; The Romanian Orthodox Episcopate of Amer-
ica: p. 104; St. Mary's Romanian Orthodox Church, Cleveland, Ohio: pp. 13,
30–31, 45, 63, 73, 75; Mark Stein Studios: p. 18; Katrina Thomas: p. 82; UPI/
Bettmann Newsphotos: pp. 89, 90, 94; Yale University: p. 93

ARTHUR DIAMOND was born in Queens, New York, and has lived and worked in New Mexico, Colorado, and Oregon. He received a degree in English literature from the University of Oregon and is presently enrolled in the graduate English program at Queens College. This is his first book.

DANIEL PATRICK MOYNIHAN is the senior United States senator from New York. He is also the only person in American history to serve in the cabinets or subcabinets of four successive presidents—Kennedy, Johnson, Nixon, and Ford. Formerly a professor of government at Harvard University, he has written and edited many books, including *Beyond the Melting Pot, Ethnicity: Theory and Experience* (both with Nathan Glazer), *Loyalties,* and *Family and Nation.*